Unleash your potential with

self-coaching

Self-Coaching refers to the process of coaching ourselves to achieve our goals, improve our performance, and overcome challenges. It involves setting goals, creating a plan to achieve them, acting, and reflecting on your progress.

- Self-awareness: Coaching ourself requires us to become more self-aware. We need to take the time to reflect on our thoughts, feelings, and behaviours. This will help us better understand ourself and our motivations.
- Accountability: When we are our own coach, we are responsible for holding ourself accountable. This means that we will need to set goals, create plans, and track our progress. By doing this, we will be more likely to follow through on our commitments and achieve our desired outcomes.
- Flexibility: Being our own coach allows us to be more flexible in our approach. We can adjust our strategies and tactics as needed to meet our changing needs and circumstances.
- Empowerment: Coaching ourself can be empowering. It puts us in the driver's seat of our own personal and professional development. By taking ownership of our growth and development, we are better able to achieve our goals and create the life we want.
- Cost-effective: Finally, being our own coach can be cost-effective. We do not need to hire a professional coach or attend expensive workshops or training programs. Instead, we can develop the skills and strategies we need to coach ourself, and apply them to our daily life.

Overall, self-coaching is a powerful tool for personal growth and development. It allows us to take control of our own success and become more self-sufficient, self-aware, and empowered.

INDEX

1. Understanding My Goals

What are my current goals and why they are important to me.

What are some potential obstacles or challenges I may encounter along the way?

What resources or support do I need in order to achieve my goals, and how can I go about obtaining them?

How will I measure my progress towards my goals, and what specific indicators will I use to track my success?

2. Let's do a Personal SWOT Analysis to help identify my strengths, weaknesses, opportunities, and threats

STRENGTHS

I. What are some skills or qualities that others have recognized in me as a strength?

II. What are some tasks or activities that come naturally to me, and how can I use these to achieve your goals?

III. What do I enjoy doing, and how can I incorporate these activities into my personal or professional life?

IV. What are some challenges I have overcome in the past, and what strengths did I draw upon to succeed?

V. What is some positive feedback or compliments I have received from others, and how can I use this feedback to recognize my strengths?

VI. What are some areas where I feel confident and competent, and how can I leverage these strengths to achieve my goals?

WEAKNESS

I. What are some areas where I struggle or face challenges?
II. What feedback have I received from others about areas where I need to improve
III. What are some common mistakes or errors I have made in the past?
IV. What are some situations or tasks that make me feel uncomfortable or anxious
V. What are some areas where I lack knowledge or experience
VI. What are some habits or behaviours that may be holding me back from achieving my goals

OPPORTUNITIES

I. What are some current trends or changes in my industry or field, and how can I leverage these to create new opportunities?

II. What are some challenges or gaps in my industry or field, and how can I develop skills or expertise to fill these gaps and create new opportunities?

III. What are some emerging technologies or innovations in my field, and how can I stay up-to-date with these developments to create new opportunities?

IV. What are some areas where my skills or experience can be applied in new and innovative ways, and how can I explore these opportunities?

V. What are some gaps or unmet needs in my personal or professional life, and how can I create new opportunities by addressing these needs?

VI. What are some networking or collaboration opportunities that can help me connect with others in my field and create new opportunities for growth and development?

THREATS

I. What are some current or potential threats to my industry or field, and how can I prepare to mitigate their impact on my work?

II. What are some potential changes or disruptions that could affect my personal or professional life, and how can I develop strategies to adapt to these changes?

III. What are some areas where I may lack expertise or knowledge, and how can I address these gaps to reduce potential threats to my work?

IV. What are some areas where I may be at risk of complacency or stagnation, and how can I challenge myself to stay motivated?

V. What are some potential conflicts or challenges I may face in my personal or professional relationships, and how can I develop strategies to address these challenges

3.1 Let me explore few questions to help improve my Adaptability Skills

Adaptability skills refer to the ability to adjust to new situations, environments, and tasks. It involves being flexible, open-minded, and willing to learn and grow. Adaptable individuals can handle change and uncertainty with ease and are able to make quick and effective adjustments when needed.

i. Example of a time when I had to **quickly adjust to a new situation** or task? How did I handle it?

ii. How do I typically **react when faced with unexpected changes** or challenges?

iii.   What strategies do I use to **cope with unexpected challenges** or obstacles in my work?

iv.   Situation where I had to **learn a new skill or technology** quickly in order to achieve a desired outcome? How did I approach the learning process and adapt to the new situation?

v.   How do I approach **working with diverse groups of people** who may have different backgrounds, experiences, or

vi. Some of the **Tools and techniques I heard** to improve Adaptability Skills?

a. **Growth mindset**: Cultivating a growth mindset involves embracing challenges, seeing failure as an opportunity for learning, and believing that skills and abilities can be developed through effort and perseverance. This mindset can help individuals approach new situations and challenges with a more positive and adaptive attitude.

b. **Resilience training**: Resilience training can help individuals develop the skills and resources needed to cope with stress and adversity, bounce back from setbacks, and adapt to changing circumstances.

c. **Exposure therapy**: Exposure therapy involves gradually exposing oneself to feared or uncomfortable situations or stimuli, in order to increase adaptability in the face of uncertainty or change.

d. **Scenario planning**: Scenario planning involves imagining and preparing for potential future scenarios, in order to develop flexible thinking and proactive adaptation strategies.

e. **Embracing diversity and inclusion**: Embracing diversity and inclusion involves actively seeking out and valuing different perspectives and backgrounds, in order to develop a more adaptive and culturally competent approach to work and life.

f. **Experimentation and iteration**: Experimentation and iteration involve trying out new approaches, testing hypotheses, and refining strategies based on feedback and results

g. **Agility training**: Agility training, including exercises such as obstacle courses or agility drills, can help individuals develop physical and mental agility, as well as improve their ability to adapt to changing circumstances.

<u>Steps I intend to take</u>

General Activities (performing new tasks, taking on new projects, and solving problems in the workplace.)

70%

Mentoring & Coaching (social interactions and collaborations with others, such as feedback, mentoring, coaching, and learning from colleagues)

20%

Workshops, Books, Videos (workshops, classes, online courses, and other structured learning experiences)

10%

3.2 Let me explore few questions to help improve my Analytical Thinking

Analytical thinking skills involve the ability to break down complex information into smaller parts, identify patterns and relationships, and use logic and reasoning to draw conclusions. These skills are crucial for problem-solving, decision-making, and critical analysis in a wide range of fields, from business to science and beyond.

i. How do I **break down complex problems** or information into smaller parts? What is the process?

ii. What **patterns do I see** in the data or information I am analysing? Are there any trends or outliers that stand out?

iii.   How do I **test my assumptions and conclusions**? Are there any other sources of information or perspectives that I could consider?

iv.   How do I **prioritize information** when analysing a situation? What criteria do I use to determine what information is most important?

v.   How do I **evaluate the potential risks and benefits** of different options when deciding? Are there any trade-offs that I need to consider?

vi. Some of the **Tools and techniques** I heard to improve analytical thinking.

a. **SWOT Analysis:** SWOT analysis helps you to evaluate the strengths, weaknesses, opportunities, and threats related to a particular situation or decision. You can identify the pros and cons of different options and make informed decisions.

b. **Cause-and-Effect Analysis:** A tool used to identify the relationship between different factors and their effects on an outcome. By using this tool, you can identify the root cause of a problem and develop effective solutions.

c. **The 5 Whys:** The 5 Whys is a technique used to identify the root cause of a problem by asking "why" five times. By using this technique, you can identify the underlying cause of a problem and develop effective solutions.

d. **Fishbone Diagram:** Fishbone diagrams are a visual tool that helps you to identify the root causes of a problem. By using this tool, you can analyse the different factors that contribute to a problem and identify potential solutions.

e. **Scenario Planning:** Scenario planning is a strategic planning tool that helps you to identify potential scenarios and outcomes based on different assumptions. You can prepare for different possibilities and make more informed decisions.

f. **Six Thinking Hats:** The Six Thinking Hats technique involves using different colored hats to represent different types of thinking (such as critical, creative, and analytical). By using this technique, you can explore different perspectives and develop more effective solutions to problems.

Steps I intend to take

General Activities (performing new tasks, taking on new projects, and solving problems in the workplace.)

70%

Mentoring & Coaching (social interactions and collaborations with others, such as feedback, mentoring, coaching, and learning from colleagues)

20%

Workshops, Books, Videos (workshops, classes, online courses, and other structured learning experiences)

10%

3.3 Let me explore few questions to help improve my Business Acumen

Business acumen refers to the ability to understand and make sound decisions in various business situations, such as identifying opportunities, managing risks, analyzing financial data, and implementing strategies to achieve goals. It involves a combination of skills, knowledge, and experience in areas such as finance, marketing, operations, and leadership.

i. What are the **key performance indicators (KPIs)** that are most important to our company/business, and how are they currently being tracked and measured?

ii. What **financial metrics** should I be monitoring to ensure the long-term sustainability of our company/business, and how can I act based on those metrics?

iii. How am I currently **identifying new business opportunities**, and what methods could I explore to improve my approach?

iv. How do I **prioritize and allocate resources** to different projects or initiatives, and what criteria do I use to make those decisions?

v. How do I **identify and manage risks** that could impact the success of our business, and what steps can I take to mitigate those risks?

vi.   Some of the **Tools and techniques** I heard to improve business acumen skills.

    a. **Industry research:** Conducting research on your industry and competitors can provide valuable insights into market trends, opportunities, and challenges.

    b. **Financial analysis:** Learning to read and interpret financial statements and ratios can help you understand the financial health of your company and make informed decisions.

    c. **Cross-functional collaboration:** Working with colleagues from different departments can help you gain a broader understanding of how your business operates and how different functions contribute to its success.

    d. **Scenario planning:** Creating and analysing hypothetical scenarios can help you anticipate potential risks and opportunities and develop contingency plans.

    e. **Business simulations:** Participating in business simulations can provide a low-risk environment to practice decision-making and develop strategic thinking skills.

    f. **SWOT analysis:** Conducting a SWOT (Strengths, Weaknesses, Opportunities, and Threats) analysis can help you assess your company's internal and external factors and identify areas for improvement.

    g. **Risk management:** Developing effective risk management strategies can help you mitigate potential threats and minimize negative impacts on your business.

Steps I intend to take

General Activities (performing new tasks, taking on new projects, and solving problems in the workplace.)

70%

Mentoring & Coaching (social interactions and collaborations with others, such as feedback, mentoring, coaching, and learning from colleagues)

20%

Workshops, Books, Videos (workshops, classes, online courses, and other structured learning experiences)

10%

3.4 Let me explore few questions to help improve my Communication Skills

Effective communication skills are crucial in personal and professional life. They enable individuals to express themselves clearly, understand others better, build strong relationships, and achieve their goals. Good communication skills can lead to better collaboration, increased productivity, and a positive impact on overall well-being

i. In what situations **do I feel most challenged** or uncomfortable in my communication?

ii. What **communication-related challenges** or obstacles do I currently face in my personal or professional life?

iii.   What **feedback have I received** in the past about my communication style?

iv.   How would I describe my **current communication style?**

v.   How do I **manage nervousness or anxiety** when communicating in front of others?

vi. Some of the **Tools and techniques** I heard to improve communication skills

a. **Practice active listening:** Focusing on the person speaking, asking questions, and reflecting on what they are saying to better understand their perspective.

b. **Record yourself:** Help you identify verbal habits or patterns that you might not be aware of, and give you an opportunity to practice and improve your tone and pacing.

c. **Join a public speaking club:** Clubs like Toastmasters provide opportunities to practice speaking in front of an audience and receive constructive feedback from peers.

d. **Use feedback:** Solicit feedback from peers, mentors, or coaches to get a better understanding of your strengths and weaknesses in communication and how to improve.

e. **Read widely:** Reading can help you expand your vocabulary, learn about different styles of communication, and become more articulate.

f. **Observe others:** How effective communicators speak, listen, and use nonverbal cues to convey their message.

g. **Attend networking events:** Opportunities to practice your communication skills in a professional setting, and can help build relationships with others in your industry.

h. **Develop your nonverbal communication skills:** Your body language, facial expressions, and tone of voice can all convey important messages. Practice using nonverbal cues effectively to support and enhance your verbal communication.

Steps I intend to take

General Activities (performing new tasks, taking on new projects, and solving problems in the workplace.)

70%

Mentoring & Coaching (social interactions and collaborations with others, such as feedback, mentoring, coaching, and learning from colleagues)

20%

Workshops, Books, Videos (workshops, classes, online courses, and other structured learning experiences)

10%

3.5 Let me explore few questions to help improve my Creativity & Innovation

Creativity and innovation skills involve generating new ideas and implementing them effectively. Creativity requires thinking outside the box and finding novel solutions, while innovation involves adding value and solving problems by turning creative ideas into practical solutions.

i. How do I typically **generate new ideas?**

ii. How do I typically **evaluate the feasibility of new ideas?**

iii.   How do I typically **implement creative ideas in a practical and effective way?** Are there any barriers that I encounter in this process?

iv.   How do I typically **handle situations where my creative ideas conflict** with existing processes or procedures?

v.   How do I typically **stay up-to-date with trends** and emerging technologies? Are there any ways that I could stay more informed?

vi. Some of the **Tools and techniques** I heard to improve creativity & innovation skills.

    a. **Brainstorming:** Generating a list of as many potential ideas as possible without evaluating them initially. This can help generate a wide range of potential ideas.

    b. **Reverse brainstorming:** Identifying potential ways to make a problem worse instead of better. This can help to identify potential solutions to the problem.

    c. **Design thinking:** This is a human-centered approach to problem-solving that involves understanding the needs and perspectives of the people affected by the problem. This help to develop solutions that are more effective and sustainable.

    d. **Prototyping:** This involves creating a physical or digital representation of an idea in order to test and refine it. This can help to identify potential flaws or opportunities for improvement and develop more effective solutions.

    e. **SCAMMPERR:** This is an acronym that stands for Substitute, Combine, Adapt, Modify, Put to another use, Eliminate, Rearrange, and Reverse. This technique can help to generate new ideas and explore different possibilities.

    f. **6-3-5 Brainwriting:** This is a technique that involves generating 108 new ideas in just 30 minutes, by having each person in a group of six generate three ideas, and then pass them to the next person who generates three more ideas based on the previous ideas.

    g. **Divergent thinking:** This involves generating as many different ideas as possible without evaluating them initially.

<u>Steps I intend to take</u>

70%

General Activities (performing new tasks, taking on new projects, and solving problems in the workplace.)

20%

Mentoring & Coaching (social interactions and collaborations with others, such as feedback, mentoring, coaching, and learning from colleagues)

10%

Workshops, Books, Videos (workshops, classes, online courses, and other structured learning experiences)

3.6 Let me explore few questions to help improve my *Customer-Oriented Skills*

Customer-oriented skills are abilities that enable individuals to understand, anticipate and meet the needs of customers. These skills include effective communication, active listening, empathy, problem-solving, conflict resolution, time management, adaptability, and product knowledge. They are crucial for building strong customer relationships, enhancing customer satisfaction, and achieving business objectives through customer-centric strategies.

i.   How well do I **understand the needs and expectations** of my customers?

ii.   What can I do to **create a more positive and memorable experience** for my customers?

iii. How can I **demonstrate a sense of urgency and responsiveness** to customers' needs and concerns?

iv. What strategies can I use to **actively listen to my customers** and better understand their needs?

v. What **feedback have I received** from customers in the past, and how can I use this feedback to improve my customer-oriented skills?

vi.   Some of the **Tools and techniques** I heard to improve customer-oriented skills.

a. **Customer feedback tools** such as surveys, online reviews, and feedback forms can help you understand customer needs and expectations.

b. **Customer journey mapping** can help you visualize the customer experience and identify areas for improvement.

c. **Self-service tools** such as chatbots, knowledge bases, and FAQs help customers find solutions to their problems quickly

d. **Net Promoter Score (NPS)** surveys can help you measure customer loyalty and satisfaction, and identify opportunities for improvement.

e. **Customer loyalty programs** can incentivize customers to return and continue doing business with you.

f. **Customer advocacy programs** can encourage satisfied customers to promote your business to others.

g. **Voice of the customer (VOC) programs** can help you gather and analyse feedback from customers to improve the customer experience.

h. **Employee engagement and satisfaction programs** can create a positive work environment and encourage employees to provide better customer service.

i. **Customer empathy mapping** can help you better understand your customers' needs, feelings, and experiences.

j. **Emotional intelligence** training can help you develop skills such as self-awareness, self-regulation, social awareness, and relationship management, which are crucial for effective customer service.

Steps I intend to take

General Activities (performing new tasks, taking on new projects, and solving problems in the workplace.)

70%

Mentoring & Coaching (social interactions and collaborations with others, such as feedback, mentoring, coaching, and learning from colleagues)

20%

Workshops, Books, Videos (workshops, classes, online courses, and other structured learning experiences)

10%

3.7 Let me explore few questions to help improve my Decision-Making Skills

Effective decision making is crucial for success in personal and professional life. Good decision-making skills enable individuals to identify and pursue opportunities, avoid potential pitfalls, and navigate complex situations. They also promote accountability, confidence, and personal growth.

i. What are the **most common challenges I face** when making decisions?

ii. How do I **gather and evaluate information** when making decisions?

iii.   How do I **measure the success** of my decisions?

iv.   Are there any **specific types of decisions** that I struggle with or find particularly challenging?

v.   How do I **manage and prioritize information** when deciding?

vi. Some of the **Tools and techniques** I heard to improve Decision-Making Skills

a. **Pros and cons:** Write down the advantages and disadvantages of each option you are considering to help evaluate and compare them.

b. **Six thinking hats:** Use Edward de Bono's approach, which involves considering decisions from different perspectives represented by six different "thinking hats".

c. **Devil's advocate:** Assign someone to challenge the assumptions and opinions of the group, to help prevent groupthink and encourage critical thinking.

d. **Decision matrix:** Create a table with criteria you consider important, rate each option on each criterion, and calculate a score for each option to help make decision.

e. **SWOT analysis:** Identify the strengths, weaknesses, opportunities, and threats of each option to help evaluate its potential outcomes.

f. **Mind mapping:** Create a visual diagram to explore different options, their connections, and potential consequences.

g. **Pareto analysis:** Identify the most significant factors influencing the decision, prioritize them, and focus on addressing the vital few to help make decision.

h. **Cost-benefit analysis:** Weigh the costs and benefits of each option to determine the most cost-effective decision.

i. **Scenario planning:** Consider different scenarios and their potential outcomes to help prepare for unexpected situations.

<u>Steps I intend to take</u>

General Activities (performing new tasks, taking on new projects, and solving problems in the workplace.)

70%

Mentoring & Coaching (social interactions and collaborations with others, such as feedback, mentoring, coaching, and learning from colleagues)

20%

Workshops, Books, Videos (workshops, classes, online courses, and other structured learning experiences)

10%

3.8 Let me explore few questions to help improve my Domain Knowledge

Domain knowledge refers to expertise or understanding of a specific subject or industry. It includes knowledge of key concepts, practices, and terminology, as well as an understanding of common challenges and opportunities within the domain. This knowledge can be gained through education, training, or experience.

i. What resources do I currently use to **stay up-to-date** with developments in my domain?

ii. What are some **recent trends or changes** I've noticed in my domain, and how do I think they will affect my work?

iii. What are **some of the gaps in my current domain knowledge**, and how can I fill those gaps?

iv. What are some **emerging technologies or practices** in my domain, and how can I stay ahead of the curve?

v. What are some **networking opportunities** that I can take advantage of to learn more about my domain and connect with other experts?

vi. Some of the **Tools and techniques** I heard to improve domain knowledge

  a. **Read industry publications and news**: Stay up-to-date with the latest developments and trends in your industry by reading publications and news sources. Subscribe to relevant newsletters and RSS feeds to get the latest information

  b. **Attend industry events and conferences**: Attend events and conferences related to your industry to network with other experts and learn about new products, and best practices

  c. **Participate in online forums and communities**: Join online forums and communities related to your industry to ask questions, share your knowledge, and learn from others.

  d. **Network with other experts**: Connect with other experts in your industry through social media, LinkedIn, or industry associations to build relationships and learn from them

  e. **Conduct research and analysis**: Conduct research and analysis on industry trends, data, and best practices to gain a deeper understanding of your domain and identify opportunities for improvement.

  f. **Read case studies**: Read case studies related to your domain to learn from real-world examples of successful and unsuccessful practices.

  g. **Participate in cross-functional projects**: Participating in cross-functional projects can help you gain a broader perspective on your domain and learn from others outside your area of expertise.

Steps I intend to take

General Activities (performing new tasks, taking on new projects, and solving problems in the workplace.)

70%

Mentoring & Coaching (social interactions and collaborations with others, such as feedback, mentoring, coaching, and learning from colleagues)

20%

Workshops, Books, Videos (workshops, classes, online courses, and other structured learning experiences)

10%

3.9 Let me explore few questions to help improve my Execution Skills

Execution skills refer to the ability to implement plans and strategies effectively and efficiently. It involves setting clear goals, prioritizing tasks, managing resources, and adapting to changes. Strong execution skills require attention to detail, time management, problem-solving, communication, and teamwork to achieve desired outcomes.

i. What specific actions can I take to **break down complex tasks into smaller, more manageable steps?**

ii. What are some **potential roadblocks or obstacles** that could prevent me from executing effectively, and how can I plan for them in advance?

iii. How can I **measure progress and track results** to ensure that I am staying on track and achieving my goals?

iv. What are some techniques that I can use to **manage risks and plan for contingencies,** especially when working on complex or high-stakes projects?

v. How can I **leverage technology and other tools** to improve my execution and streamline my workflow?

vi. Some of the **Tools and techniques** I heard to improve execution skills.

   a. **Action plans:** Breaking down complex projects or goals into smaller, more manageable steps and creating a detailed action plan with deadlines can help you stay organized and on track.

   b. **Prioritization techniques:** Using tools like the Eisenhower Matrix or the Pareto Principle can help you prioritize tasks and focus on what is most important.

   c. **Time management tools:** Tools like calendars, to-do lists, and time-tracking apps can help you manage your time effectively and ensure that you are using it efficiently.

   d. **Risk management tools:** Techniques like risk identification, risk analysis, and risk mitigation can help anticipate and manage potential obstacles that could impact execution.

   e. **Continuous improvement:** Techniques like Lean Six Sigma, Kaizen, or Agile methodologies can help you continuously improve your processes and workflows to optimize execution and achieve better results.

   f. **Feedback mechanisms:** Soliciting feedback from team members, colleagues, and stakeholders can help you identify areas for improvement and adjust to improve execution.

   g. **Performance metrics:** Establishing key performance indicators (KPIs) and tracking them over time can help you measure progress and identify areas for improvement.

   h. **Time blocking:** Scheduling specific blocks of time for tasks or projects can help you stay focused and avoid distractions.

Steps I intend to take

General Activities (performing new tasks, taking on new projects, and solving problems in the workplace.)

70%

Mentoring & Coaching (social interactions and collaborations with others, such as feedback, mentoring, coaching, and learning from colleagues)

20%

Workshops, Books, Videos (workshops, classes, online courses, and other structured learning experiences)

10%

3.10 Let me explore few questions to help improve my Interpersonal Skills

Interpersonal skills are the abilities that allow individuals to communicate, interact, and work effectively with others. These skills include active listening, empathy, collaboration, conflict resolution, and assertiveness, among others. Having strong interpersonal skills can help individuals build positive relationships, navigate social situations, and succeed in various personal and professional settings.

i. Are there any **specific individuals or types of people** that I struggle to communicate effectively with? Why do I think this is the case?

ii. How do I handle situations where **someone disagrees** with me or has a different perspective?

iii. How do I **manage my emotions** in challenging interpersonal situations?

iv. How do I **show empathy and understanding towards others?** Are there any ways I could improve my ability to see situations from their perspective?

v. What kind of **feedback I receive** from others about my interpersonal skills?

vi. Some of the **Tools and techniques** I heard to improve Interpersonal skills

a. **Active Listening:** This involves paying full attention to the person speaking, acknowledging their message, and responding thoughtfully. This helps build trust and understanding in relationships.

b. **Empathy:** The ability to understand and feel the emotions of others. It involves putting yourself in the shoes of the other person, understanding their point of view, and showing them that you care.

c. **Nonverbal Communication:** It includes body language, facial expressions, and tone of voice, which can all communicate meaning beyond words. Paying attention to nonverbal cues can help understand others and communicate effectively.

d. **Emotional Intelligence:** This involves understanding and managing your own emotions, as well as recognizing and responding to the emotions of others. It can help you build stronger relationships and navigate social situations

e. **Feedback:** Seeking feedback from others on your interpersonal skills can help you identify areas for improvement and make changes accordingly.

f. **Self-reflection:** Our interactions with others, and identifying areas where you may have struggled or succeeded, can help you develop a deeper understanding of your interpersonal skills and how you can improve them.

g. **Peer mentoring:** Participating in peer mentoring programs can help you build relationships with others and learn new interpersonal skills from your peers.

<u>Steps I intend to take</u>

General Activities *(performing new tasks, taking on new projects, and solving problems in the workplace.)*

70%

Mentoring & Coaching *(social interactions and collaborations with others, such as feedback, mentoring, coaching, and learning from colleagues)*

20%

Workshops, Books, Videos *(workshops, classes, online courses, and other structured learning experiences)*

10%

3.11 Let me explore few questions to help improve my Negotiation Skills

Negotiation skills are important for resolving conflicts, improving communication, achieving goals, and saving time and money. They involve effective communication, active listening, and understanding the other party's perspective.

i. How do I typically **prepare for a negotiation?** What steps could I take to improve my preparation process?

ii. How do I approach **difficult or challenging negotiations?** What strategies have worked well for me in the past?

iii.   How do I approach negotiating with someone **who has more power or authority than me?** What strategies could I use to effectively negotiate in these situations?

iv.   How do I **evaluate the success of a negotiation?** What criteria do I use to measure the effectiveness of the negotiation?

v.   How do I ensure that I am **communicating clearly and effectively during a negotiation?** What strategies could I use to improve my communication skills?

vi.   Some of the **Tools and techniques** I heard to improve negotiation skills.

   a.   **Preparation:** Before entering a negotiation, take the time to research the other party, identify your goals and priorities, and consider potential obstacles or challenges.

   b.   **Active listening:** Active listening and an understanding of the other party's needs and interests. Practice listening carefully to what the other party is saying and ask questions to clarify their position.

   c.   **Building rapport:** Using small talk or finding common ground to establish a connection with the other party.

   d.   **Understanding our BATNA:** (Best Alternative to a Negotiated Agreement) is our next option if a negotiation fails. Understanding our BATNA can help us determine our negotiation leverage and identify our bottom line. It can also help us decide when to walk away from a negotiation.

   e.   **Using objective criteria:** such as market data or industry standards, can help support your negotiation position and make your argument more compelling.

   f.   **Using the "anchoring" technique:** It involves making an initial offer that is higher or lower than your actual desired outcome, with the intention of influencing the other party's perception of what is reasonable.

   g.   **Practicing negotiation scenarios:** Practicing negotiation scenarios with a friend or colleague can help you develop your negotiation skills in a low-pressure environment. It can also help you identify areas for improvement and refine your negotiation strategy.

Steps I intend to take

General Activities (performing new tasks, taking on new projects, and solving problems in the workplace.)

70%

Mentoring & Coaching (social interactions and collaborations with others, such as feedback, mentoring, coaching, and learning from colleagues)

20%

Workshops, Books, Videos (workshops, classes, online courses, and other structured learning experiences)

10%

3.12 Let me explore few questions to help improve my Peer Relationship

Peer relationships are important for personal growth, socialization, and emotional support. They allow individuals to develop social skills, explore different aspects of themselves, and find validation for their beliefs and values. Peers can provide learning opportunities, new perspectives, and networking opportunities that can help individuals achieve their goals

i. What are my current peer relationships like, and how do they impact my work and my overall well-being?

ii. How do I typically approach conflict with peers, and what strategies have worked well for me in the past

iii.   How do I **communicate with my peers**, and what techniques can I use to improve my communication skills?

iv.   What are some **shared interests or activities** that I and my peers can engage in to build stronger connections?

v.   What **boundaries do I need to set** in my peer relationships to maintain a healthy balance and respect for myself and

vi. Some of the **Tools and techniques** I heard to improve peer relationships

a. **Shared interests:** Find shared interests or activities that you and your peers can engage in together. This can help build stronger connections and provide opportunities for positive interactions.

b. **Gratitude and appreciation**: Show gratitude and appreciation for your peers, and the positive impact they have on your life. A simple thank you or compliment can go a long way in building relationships.

c. **Conflict resolution:** Address conflicts or misunderstandings that may arise in a respectful and constructive way. Focus on finding solutions and compromise, rather than placing blame.

d. **Feedback:** Offer constructive feedback to your peers in a way that is helpful and not hurtful. Be specific and provide actionable advice to help them improve.

e. **Accountability**: Set shared goals with your peers and hold each other accountable to achieve them. This can help build a sense of responsibility and teamwork.

f. **Shared experiences**: Create opportunities for shared experiences with your peers, such as group projects, volunteering, or social events. These experiences can help build stronger connections and positive memories.

g. **Support networks:** Seek out support networks, such as clubs or organizations, that can provide a sense of community and belonging.

Steps I intend to take

General Activities (performing new tasks, taking on new projects, and solving problems in the workplace.)

70%

Mentoring & Coaching (social interactions and collaborations with others, such as feedback, mentoring, coaching, and learning from colleagues)

20%

Workshops, Books, Videos (workshops, classes, online courses, and other structured learning experiences)

10%

3.13 Let me explore few questions to help improve my People Development Skills

Developing team competency involves building and enhancing the collective skills and knowledge of a team to achieve common goals through effective communication, collaboration, problem-solving, and trust. It improves team performance, productivity, and culture, leading to greater success and satisfaction.

i. What **challenges have I noticed within my team**, and how can developing their skills and knowledge help address those challenges?

ii. How do I currently **assess the competency of my team**, and what areas do I think they need to improve on?

iii. How can I **encourage my team to take ownership** of their own development, and drive their own growth?

iv. How can I create a **culture of continuous learning** and improvement within my team?

v. How do I currently **provide feedback to my team members**, and how can I make that feedback more effective and constructive to support their development?

vi.   Some of the **Tools and techniques** I heard to enhance people development skills.

    a. **Coaching and Mentoring**: Providing individualized coaching and mentoring to team members can help them identify their strengths and weaknesses, set development goals, and receive personalized guidance and feedback.

    b. **Team Building Activities**: Organizing team-building activities such as outdoor retreats, team lunches, or social events can help build relationships and trust among team members

    c. **Performance Metrics and Feedback**: It can help team members track their progress and identify areas for improvement, as well as provide managers with insights into team development needs.

    d. **Continuous Learning**: Encouraging team members to pursue ongoing learning and development through courses, conferences, or other opportunities can promote a culture of continuous learning and improvement within the team.

    e. **Action Learning**: It combines problem-solving and group learning, where team members work together to solve a real-world problem, and learn from the experience.

    f. **Shadowing and Job Shadowing**: Observing a colleague in their role, while job shadowing involves spending a day in their shoes. These experiences can help team members gain new insights and perspectives, and develop new skills.

    g. **Knowledge Management**: Developing a knowledge management system can help capture and share institutional knowledge within the team, improving learning and development opportunities for all members.

Steps I intend to take

General Activities (performing new tasks, taking on new projects, and solving problems in the workplace.)

70%

Mentoring & Coaching (social interactions and collaborations with others, such as feedback, mentoring, coaching, and learning from colleagues)

20%

Workshops, Books, Videos (workshops, classes, online courses, and other structured learning experiences)

10%

3.14 Let me explore few questions to help improve my Planning Skills

Planning skills involve the ability to create effective strategies, set goals, prioritize tasks, organize resources, and anticipate and manage risks. It involves being proactive, adaptable, and focused on achieving desired outcomes in a timely and efficient manner.

i. A **recent situation** where my planning skills was challenged?

ii. What **obstacles do I face** when planning?

iii. What are the **consequences of not planning properly**, and how does it impact my productivity and performance?

iv. How do I **determine which tasks or projects to prioritize**, and what criteria do I use to make those decisions?

v. How can I **leverage technology and other tools** to enhance my planning skills and improve my productivity?

vi. Some of the **Tools and techniques** I heard to improve planning skills.

    a. **Time management** tools, such as calendars, to-do lists, and reminder apps

    b. **Goal-setting frameworks**, such as SMART or OKRs, to help define specific and achievable objectives

    c. **SWOT analysis or risk management tools**, such as Excel or Google Sheets, to help identify potential challenges and plan for contingencies

    d. **Prioritization techniques**, such as the Eisenhower Matrix or ABC analysis, help identify important tasks or projects

    e. **Personal Kanban:** a visual method for organizing tasks and activities using a board and cards to represent different stages of work, such as "to do", "in progress", and "done". It can help improve workflow, increase focus, and reduce stress by providing a clear picture of priorities and progress

    f. **Decision-making frameworks**, such as cost-benefit analysis or the 6 Thinking Hats, to help weigh different options and make informed choices

    g. **Performance metrics and tracking tools**, such as Key Performance Indicators (KPIs) or Balanced Scorecards, to help measure progress and identify areas for improvement

    h. **Standard Operating Procedures (SOPs),** to help establish consistency and streamline processes in the planning and execution of tasks or projects.

    i. **Gantt charts**: a graphical representation of a project schedule that helps to visualize and track progress over time.

<u>Steps I intend to take</u>

General Activities (performing new tasks, taking on new projects, and solving problems in the workplace.)

70%

Mentoring & Coaching (social interactions and collaborations with others, such as feedback, mentoring, coaching, and learning from colleagues)

20%

Workshops, Books, Videos (workshops, classes, online courses, and other structured learning experiences)

10%

3.15 Let me explore few questions to help improve my Problem-Solving Skills

Problem-solving skills refer to the ability to identify, analyse, and solve problems in a systematic and effective manner. This includes the ability to break down complex problems into smaller, more manageable components, analyse the root cause of the problem, generate, and evaluate potential solutions, and implement the most appropriate solution

i.   How do I typically **approach a problem-solving situation?** What steps do I take?

ii. What **obstacles do I typically encounter** when trying to solve a problem?

iii. How do I typically handle a situation where I **do not know the answer** or solution to a problem?

iv. How do I typically **prioritize potential solutions** to a problem? What factors do I consider when making this decision?

v. How do I ensure that the solution I choose to a **problem is sustainable over the long-term?** What steps do I take to ensure that the problem does not recur in the future?

vi. Some of the **Tools and techniques** I heard to improve problem-solving skills.

a. **Brainstorming**: Generating a list of as many potential solutions as possible without evaluating them initially.

b. **Root cause analysis**: By addressing the root cause of the problem, one can prevent the problem from recurring

c. **SWOT analysis**: This involves analysing the strengths, weaknesses, opportunities, and threats related to a problem. This can help to identify potential solutions and assess their feasibility.

d. **Fishbone diagram**: This involves identifying the different factors that contribute to a problem and mapping them out in a structured way.

e. **Decision matrix**: Evaluating potential solutions based on multiple criteria, such as cost, feasibility, and impact.

f. **Pareto analysis**: Identifying the 20% of causes that lead to 80% of the problems. By focusing on the most significant causes, you can address the underlying issues effectively.

g. **5 Whys**: This involves asking "why" five times to identify the root cause of a problem. This can help to uncover the underlying issues and develop effective solutions.

h. **Design thinking**: This is a human-cantered approach to problem-solving that involves understanding the needs and perspectives of the people affected by the problem.

i. **Kaizen**: It involves making small, incremental changes to a process or system over time. This can help to identify and address problems proactively, before they become more significant.

<u>Steps I intend to take</u>

General Activities (performing new tasks, taking on new projects, and solving problems in the workplace.)

70%

Mentoring & Coaching (social interactions and collaborations with others, such as feedback, mentoring, coaching, and learning from colleagues)

20%

Workshops, Books, Videos (workshops, classes, online courses, and other structured learning experiences)

10%

3.16 Let me explore few questions to help improve my Result Oriented Skills

Result-oriented refers to an approach or mindset that focuses on achieving specific outcomes or goals. It involves setting clear objectives and developing strategies and actions that are aligned with those objectives. A result-oriented person is driven by measurable progress and strives to continuously improve their performance to achieve better outcomes.

i. What is the **most important result** I want to achieve right now and why it is important for me?

ii. What **steps do I need** to take to achieve this result?

iii.   What are the **potential roadblocks or challenges** I may encounter in achieving this result?

iv.   What specific **skills do I need to develop** to become more result-oriented?

v.   What **metrics can I use** to track my progress towards my goals? How can I use **data and analytics** to make more informed decisions and improve my results?

vi. Some of the **Tools and techniques** I heard to improve result-oriented skills.

a. **Goal-setting frameworks** such as SMART goals, OKRs (Objectives and Key Results), and BHAGs (Big Hairy Audacious Goals) can help set clear & measurable objectives.

b. **Time management techniques** such as the Pomodoro Technique, Time Blocking, and Eisenhower Matrix help you prioritize tasks and manage your time more effectively.

c. **Collaboration and networking** can help you leverage the knowledge and expertise of others to achieve outcomes.

d. **SWOT analysis** help you identify your strengths, weaknesses, opportunities, and threats, and use that information to develop strategies for achieving better results.

e. **Feedback and evaluation tools** such as 360-degree feedback or performance reviews can provide valuable insights

f. **Continuous improvement** methodologies such as Lean Six Sigma or Agile can help you identify and eliminate inefficiencies and improve your processes over time.

g. **Decision-making frameworks** such as the SWOT analysis, the Pros and Cons list, or the Decision Matrix help make more informed decisions that are aligned with your goals.

h. **Project management tools** such as Gantt charts or Kanban boards can help organize and prioritize tasks and projects to achieve better results.

i. **Learning from failure** through techniques such as post-mortem analysis or failure mode and effects analysis (FMEA) can help identify the root causes of failures and prevent them from happening again in the future

<u>Steps I intend to take</u>

General Activities (performing new tasks, taking on new projects, and solving problems in the workplace.)

70%

Mentoring & Coaching (social interactions and collaborations with others, such as feedback, mentoring, coaching, and learning from colleagues)

20%

Workshops, Books, Videos (workshops, classes, online courses, and other structured learning experiences)

10%

3.17 Let me explore few questions to help improve my Strategic Thinking

Strategic thinking is the ability to analyze complex situations, anticipate potential outcomes, and develop creative solutions that align with long-term goals. It involves considering multiple perspectives, identifying trends and patterns, and making informed decisions to achieve a competitive advantage in a rapidly changing environment.

i.   What are some of the **common challenges I face** when trying to develop a strategic mindset?

ii. Example of when I had to **lead others in developing and implementing a strategic plan**, and what did I learn from this experience?

iii. How do I gather and **analyze data to inform my strategic decision-making**, and how can I improve my skills in this area?

iv. How can I develop my ability to **identify patterns and trends in data**, and use this information to make informed decisions?

v. How can I **measure and track the impact** of my strategic initiatives, and adjust my approach based on feedback and

vi. Some of the **Tools and techniques** I heard to improve strategic thinking ability

a. **SWOT Analysis:** By conducting a SWOT analysis, we can identify areas where we need to improve, and areas where we can capitalize on opportunities.

b. **Scenario Planning:** It involves creating different scenarios or possible futures based on different assumptions and drivers of change. By considering different scenarios, we can prepare for a range of possible outcomes

c. **PEST Analysis:** It is a framework for assessing external factors that can impact an organization or industry, including political, economic, social, and technological factors. By analyzing these factors, we can identify trends and potential risks or opportunities.

d. **Benchmarking:** Benchmarking involves comparing an organization's performance or processes to those of other organizations or industries.

e. **Porter's Five Forces:** It helps us understand the competitive forces within our industry or market. By analyzing these forces, we can identify potential threats and opportunities, and develop strategy.

f. **Value Chain Analysis:** Value chain analysis is a framework for understanding how an organization creates value for its customers. By analyzing the value chain, we can identify areas where we can improve efficiency and create more value for customers.

Steps I intend to take

General Activities (performing new tasks, taking on new projects, and solving problems in the workplace.)

70%

Mentoring & Coaching (social interactions and collaborations with others, such as feedback, mentoring, coaching, and learning from colleagues)

20%

courses, and other structured learning experiences)

10%

3.18 Let me explore few questions to help improve my Stress Management Abilities

Stress management is crucial because excessive stress can have negative effects on both physical and mental health. By learning to manage stress effectively, individuals can reduce the risk of developing chronic illnesses and improve their overall well-being and quality of life.

i. What are some of the **biggest sources of stress** in my life currently?

ii. How do I **recognize when I am feeling stressed**? What physical or emotional signals do I experience?

iii.   What are some **stress management techniques or strategies** that I have tried in the past?

iv.   How can I **adjust my schedule or workload** to reduce stress levels?

v.   What are some **self-care activities** that I enjoy and can incorporate into my routine to reduce stress?

vi. Some of the **Tools and techniques** I heard to enhance stress management abilities.

    a. **Mindfulness meditation:** This involves focusing your attention on the present moment, and can help reduce stress and anxiety levels.

    b. **Breathing exercises:** Controlled breathing can help reduce physical tension and promote relaxation.

    c. **Physical activity:** Regular exercise can help reduce stress and boost mood.

    d. **Time management:** Prioritizing tasks and setting realistic goals can help reduce stress and increase productivity.

    e. **Relaxation techniques:** Yoga, tai chi, and progressive muscle relaxation are examples of techniques that can help reduce stress and promote relaxation.

    f. **Music therapy:** Listening to calming music or creating music can help reduce stress and promote relaxation.

    g. **Art therapy:** Such as drawing or painting, can help reduce stress and promote relaxation.

    h. **Mindful walking:** This involves walking slowly and focusing on the physical sensations of each step, which can help reduce stress and promote relaxation.

    i. **Gratitude practice:** Focusing on what you are grateful for can help shift your mindset to a more positive outlook, reducing stress and improving well-being.

    j. **Biohacking:** The use of technology to track and optimize health, such as sleep tracking or stress measurement, can help individuals manage stress more effectively.

<u>Steps I intend to take</u>

General Activities (performing new tasks, taking on new projects, and solving problems in the workplace.)

70%

Mentoring & Coaching (social interactions and collaborations with others, such as feedback, mentoring, coaching, and learning from colleagues)

20%

Workshops, Books, Videos (workshops, classes, online courses, and other structured learning experiences)

10%

3.19 Let me explore few questions to help improve my Time Management Skills

Time management skill is important because it can help us achieve your goals, reduce stress, improve decision making, balance your work and personal life, and increase accountability. By managing our time effectively, we can make the most of our available resources and achieve greater success in all areas of our life.

i. What are my **top priorities right now**, and how can I make sure I am dedicating enough time to each one?

ii. How can I **break down my daily tasks into smaller, more manageable steps** to help me stay focused and motivated?

iii.   What is my **biggest time-wasters**, and how can I eliminate them or minimize their impact on my day?

iv.   What tasks or **activities are taking up too much of my time**, and how can I delegate or eliminate them?

v.   What are the **consequences of not managing my time effectively**, and how can I use this knowledge to motivate

vi. Some of the **Tools and techniques I heard** to improve time management skills?

a. **To-do lists:** Create a list of tasks you need to complete, and prioritize them based on their importance and urgency.

b. **Time blocking:** Allocate specific time slots for each task, and work on them during those time slots.

c. **Pomodoro Technique:** Work for 25 minutes on a task, take a 5-minute break, and then repeat the cycle.

d. **Eisenhower Matrix:** Divide tasks into four quadrants based on their urgency and importance, and prioritize

e. **Calendar:** To schedule appointments, meetings, and deadlines, and set reminders to keep yourself on track.

f. **Time tracking software:** To track how much time you spend on each task, and use the data to optimize productivity.

g. **Timeboxing:** Allocate a specific amount of time to each task and work on it during that time period, without allowing any distractions or interruptions.

h. **Eliminating distractions:** Identify the things that distract you from your work, and take steps to eliminate or minimize them.

i. **Delegation:** Delegate tasks that can be handled by others, and focus on the tasks that only you can do.

j. **Batch processing:** Group similar tasks together and complete them in batches to reduce the time spent switching between different types of work.

k. **Saying no:** Learn to say no to tasks or commitments that do not align with your goals or priorities, and avoid overcommitting yourself.

<u>Steps I intend to take</u>

General Activities (performing new tasks, taking on new projects, and solving problems in the workplace.)

70%

Mentoring & Coaching (social interactions and collaborations with others, such as feedback, mentoring, coaching, and learning from colleagues)

20%

Workshops, Books, Videos (workshops, classes, online courses, and other structured learning experiences)

10%

3.20 Let me explore few questions to help improve my Upward Relationship (Reporting Manager)

Managing upward relationship refers to the ability of an employee to build and maintain a positive and productive relationship with their boss or superiors. It involves effective communication, understanding their goals and needs, and providing valuable feedback to ensure a successful working relationship.

i. What are my **reporting manager's top priorities and goals**, and how can I align my work to support them?

ii. What **communication strategies** have I found to be effective when working with my reporting manager?

iii. How can I **anticipate my reporting manager's needs** and provide proactive solutions to problems or challenges he/she may face?

iv. What **feedback have I received** from my reporting manager, and how can I use it to improve my working relationship?

v. What steps can I take to **build trust** with my reporting manager and ensure open and honest communication?

vi.   Some of the **Tools and techniques** I heard to improve Upward Relationship

    a. **Active Listening**: Practice active listening by focusing on your reporting manager's communication and responding appropriately. This technique helps build rapport and trust

    b. **Prioritize**: Understand your reporting manager's priorities and focus on delivering high-quality work that aligns with those priorities. This shows your reporting manager that you are committed to their success and can help build trust

    c. **Communication**: Communicate with your reporting manager, through email, phone, or in-person meetings. Ensure that you are clear, concise, and professional

    d. **Manage Expectations**: Manage your reporting manager's expectations by setting clear goals and timelines for your work. Be transparent about what you can/cannot deliver, and communicate any delays that may impact your work.

    e. **Collaborate**: Look for opportunities to collaborate with your reporting manager on projects or initiatives. This can help understand their working style and preferences.

    f. **Follow Through**: Follow through on your commitments and deliver high-quality work that meets or exceeds your reporting manager's expectations.

    g. **Time Management**: Use tools such as calendars and to-do list to prioritize your work and stay organized.

    h. **Empowerment**: Empower your boss by providing them with the information and resources they need to make informed decisions.

Steps I intend to take

General Activities (performing new tasks, taking on new projects, and solving problems in the workplace.)

70%

Mentoring & Coaching (social interactions and collaborations with others, such as feedback, mentoring, coaching, and learning from colleagues)

20%

Workshops, Books, Videos (workshops, classes, online courses, and other structured learning experiences)

10%

www.ingramcontent.com/pod-product-compliance
Lightning Source LLC
Chambersburg PA
CBHW031455150726
47990CB00007B/2771